Georges HATHRY

Tithe

Investing in the kingdom of heaven

ScienciaScripts

This book is a translation from the original published under ISBN 978-620-6-70602-1.

Publisher:
Sciencia Scripts
is a trademark of
Dodo Books Indian Ocean Ltd. and OmniScriptum S.R.L publishing group

120 High Road, East Finchley, London, N2 9ED, United Kingdom
Str. Armeneasca 28/1, office 1, Chisinau MD-2012, Republic of Moldova, Europe

ISBN: 978-620-7-30900-9

Georges HATHRY

The tithe

Investing in the kingdom of heaven

HATHRY GEORGES CAPITAL

The tithe

Investing in the kingdom of heaven

HATHRY Georges Capital, February 2024

Table of contents

"How good it is to celebrate our God with our songs. How good it is to praise him as he deserves."

Tithing at the Temple, by Pierre Mosnier.

"Dedicate a portion of one's income or crops to financially support a church or religious community."

PREFACE

PREFACE

One Thursday morning, Wilson RAY decided to donate part of his income to his church. His decision came after a three-day retreat at the Saint Anthony Center in Padua. During this retreat, he spent much of his time meditating on the meaning of money in the life of a Christian. The Bible verses that touched him deeply were the following:

"Do not store up for yourselves riches in this world, where worms and rust destroy...rather store up for yourselves riches in heaven where there are neither worms nor rust to destroy...For your heart will always be where your riches are." Matthew 6:19-21

"No one can serve two masters: either he will hate the first and love the second; or he will cling to the first and despise the second. You cannot serve both God and money." Matthew 6:24

After the next morning's prayer time, he felt the desire in the depths of his heart to systematically offer God the first part of any income he had from that day on. Inwardly, his heart told him that this was the only way to put God above money. He was also convinced that it was a way of thanking God for all the graces he received freely.

Is it possible to be like Wilson today? Can you decide to put God first and above money? Would it be possible for you to put God on the twelfth floor and leave your material riches on the first floor of your life's building?

I wouldn't dare answer those questions for you! But you can meditate on this subject for yourself. To help you on your way, we're going to present some small lights in this book, in the hope that they can guide you in your choice of the right master.

"I am the vine and you are the branches. He who remains united to me, and to whom I am united, bears much fruit, for you can do nothing without me." John 15:5

INTRODUCTION

INTRODUCTION

REGAIN, a young, devout Christian, used to say that money answers everything. Whenever he chatted with his friend FERNAND, he would repeat the phrase: "Money answers all". But FERNAND disagreed. For FERNAND, money was merely a means at man's disposal for the needs of life. Money was like a servant. It wasn't important above all else. Is it possible for you today to have FERNAND's point of view? Do you agree with REGAIN's opinion? Isn't your answer influenced by your own experiences and personal history?

Before tackling the subject of tithing, it's important to realize the place money and the pursuit of wealth occupy in your life. Is it money that drives your life, or is God the ideal path for you? If, at a crossroads, you were faced with a choice: one path presents money and the other presents God. One way shows you your projects, your businesses, your material possessions, and the other way presents Jesus, the son of God, who asks you to trust him, to let him lead you, to follow his path, and your projects, your businesses and your happiness will be guaranteed. Which will you choose?

"Money? Perhaps it would be more concrete and realistic as a choice to make and a path to follow for your happiness? More proactive, because you can make a precise plan to realize your projects and decide on your own what concrete actions to take to get there.

"God and his son Jesus"? Would this choice be more abstract? A more difficult path to follow? The plan would not be entirely under your control. Some say God writes straight on curved lines. And God leaves you free to make your choices. You can do as little Thérèse did when she said: *"I choose everything", meaning: "I choose whatever God wants for me. I'm not content to endure, but by a free adherence of my will, I decide to choose what I haven't chosen. Therese had this to say: "I want everything that upsets me." Outwardly, this changes nothing in the situation; but inwardly, it changes everything; this consent inspired by love and trust makes me free, active and no longer passive, and allows God to draw good from everything that happens to me, good or bad."*

Know that every day you make a choice in your life: money or God? Which master do you want to follow?

In this little book, we'll try to discover together a small way of choosing God's way in our economic life. It's also an act of putting God at the center of our finances. It's also a way of surrendering to divine providence and trusting God. This is the act of giving one's tithe. That's why this book is entitled: "Tithing: Investing in the Kingdom of Heaven". What is tithing? Why tithe? What is the history of tithing? What does the Bible say about tithing? What is the Church's opinion on tithing? Who can tithe? Who should I tithe to? What graces are attached to tithing?

To answer these questions, this book is subdivided into seven parts: part one deals with the definition and nature of tithing, part two deals with the history of tithing, part three deals with tithing and offerings, part four deals with the process of tithing, part five deals with God's people and tithing, part six deals with the fundamental choice and decision (Money or God), part seven deals with tithing for entrepreneurs and in business.

"Tithing is an act of faith that brings us closer to God".

1ère PART: DEFINITION AND NATURE OF THE TITHE

1ère PART: DEFINITION AND NATURE OF THE TAX

Chapter 1: Definition of tithing

Tithing is the historic practice of taking a percentage (usually 10%) of one's income or crops to financially support a church or religious community. It was a form of voluntary religious contribution once used in many cultures. Today, tithing is less commonly practiced, but can still be observed in some religious traditions.

The tithe or decime (from Latin: decima, "tenth") is a variable contribution, etymologically 10%, paid in kind or in cash to a civil or religious institution. Known since ancient Rome and mentioned in the Bible, this tax is used in Judaism and Christianity. It played a structuring role in Western feudal society from the High Middle Ages onwards.

In Genesis Gn 4, the story of the sacrifices of Cain and Abel evokes the offering of a share of the harvest, and the iconography of this theme in churches from the 11th century onwards is a reminder of the obligation and sacred significance of tithes in the medieval and modern West. The first mention of tithing as such in the Bible is that offered by Abram to the high priest Melchisedech in the Book of Genesis, Gen 14:18-20. Later (Gen 28:20-22), after the ladder dream, Jacob vows to give God a tenth of what God gives him.

Tithing was a religious rule well established at the time of Jesus of Nazareth, and there is no commandment on the subject in the New

Testament. Several references to tithing can be found in the Gospel of Matthew, Mt 22:23, the Gospel of Luke, Lk 11:42 and Lk 18:12, and the Epistle to the Hebrews, Heb 7:1-126. This last passage refers to Abraham's tithe paid to Melchizedek.

The tithe is defined as a tax on the production of the soil and craftsmen, intended for the Church with three shares: one for the parish, a second for the poor and the third for the clerics who serve it. In Western Europe, the Council of Tours in 567 issued a decree for the collection of tithes. In 585, the Second Council of Macon threatened those who failed to pay tithes with excommunication. Until then, tithing had been recommended and spontaneous, but from the end of the 8th century it was made compulsory by public law in the Carolingian Empire. Abolished in France by the Revolution in several stages between 1789 and 1793, it ceased to be imposed in canon law.

In Protestantism, Martin Luther considers that the law of grace excludes the law of compulsory tithing. In a sermon of August 27, 1525, he mentions Paul's passage in Galatians 5:3, which states that "if I accept to live according to the Law of Moses, I am obliged to practice the whole Law" (Deut 28:58)16. Many Protestant denominations see tithing as a non-compulsory act of generosity. Luther's Reformation was formed at the time of the German Peasants' War, and the second of the twelve articles of their manifesto denounces the misappropriation of tithes, without denying their existence.

In evangelical Christianity, positions on tithing vary from denomination to denomination. In some cases, tithing is compulsory and takes up a large part of every worship service. Promises of divine healing and prosperity are guaranteed in exchange for certain amounts of donations. Fundamentalist pastors threaten those who fail to tithe with Old Testament curses, attacks from the devil and poverty. For other evangelical churches, tithing is not an obligation, but an invitation.

In the Western Roman Church, the tithe, or rather tithes, an ecclesiastical tax from which no one was exempt, at least initially, became definitively compulsory, governed by public law and subject to state jurisdiction in 779 by decree of Charlemagne, King of the Franks and Emperor following the Assembly of Herstal, confirmed in 794 after the Synod of Frankfurt. This levy on soil production lasted for a thousand years, ending in France with the French Revolution.

Chapter 2: Nature of tithing

Several types of tithe are described in Deuteronomy Deut 14:22-29 2:3. Terumat hamaasser is taken from the produce of the harvest in the Land of Israel, i.e. the tithe of the tithe (one percent), and is given to the cohanim. The Maasser rishon, one-tenth of each year's income and produce, is given to the Levites. The Ma'asser Sheni (second tithe) consists in taking a tenth of the agricultural production of the first, second, fourth and fifth years of the septennial cycle of the land to bring to the Temple and consume there. Another tithe, Ma'asser 'Ani, is taken in the third and sixth years of the seven-year cycle. No tithe is paid in the seventh year, Shmita, as the land must be left to rest.

In the Book of Malachi Ma 3:8-12, non-observance of tithes is considered theft from God, while faithfulness to tithes promotes blessings.

The nature, operation and justification of this tax, which is in kind, is initially ecclesial.

It is also land-related, linked to the land and its production. Tithes can be sold, granted or returned, with or without the land to which they are linked; from the 12th century onwards, tithes were not systematically linked to a place of worship.

Despite its canonical justification, it was a matter of civil jurisdiction from the outset. This tax system, which lasted for a thousand years, involved decisions by provincial parliaments and the king. Necker, at the end of the 18th century, revealed the exorbitant amount of the tithe: one hundred and twenty million livres, more than the taille and capitation combined, the leading fiscal resource, it attracted a great deal of covetousness in France, then in great deficit.

Levied for the benefit of the decimator, initially the parish priest, it is divided into three parts: remuneration of the parish clerk(s), maintenance and operation of the place of worship, and relief for the poor, destitute and travelers. Some add a fourth share, that of the bishop. The bishop's share, which grew in importance at the expense of the other three shares, explains its capture by convents, ecclesiastical lords and secular lords.

Tithes relate to the production of the soil and the output of craftsmen, and concern all landowners, whatever their rank, and all those who work the soil, whatever their status. A distinction is made between gros dîmes (large tithes) on cereals and wine, and menues dîmes (small tithes) on fruit and vegetables. Charnage tithes are paid on the growth of livestock. Woods, meadows and ponds are generally exempt. It is called "solite" in Middle French "usuel" for products usually taxed, and "insolite" if the decimator claims it on a new fruit or a new production, in which case it is called "dîme novale", which becomes customary after forty years of collection. Most tithes are predial, levied on the production of the soil by the decimator or his farmer, while others are personal, levied on the work of the craftsman or on other profits.

Swivel measure in kersantite stone used to pay tithes (15th century, Musée du Léon, Lesneven)

"Render unto Caesar the things that are Caesar's, and unto God the things that are God's".

2ème PART: HISTORY OF THE TITHE

2ème PART: HISTORY OF THE TITHE

Chapter 1: Rome and tithing

In the Roman provinces, a land tax destined for Rome was levied on the products of the soil: cereals and fruit production, wine and oil. The aim was to profit from the conquest and maintain the empire's troops and civil servants. The justification was to allow these territories to benefit from the Pax Romana. The method of collection varied from province to province: foodstuffs were transported to Rome in nearby provinces, and in more distant provinces, transformed into coins paid into the treasury by publicans.

In the New Testament text, this phrase is attributed to Jesus when answering a trick question about paying taxes to the Roman emperor. The meaning of this statement is often interpreted as a separation between civil obligations and religious duties.

In essence, Jesus stresses the importance of respecting civil authorities by paying the taxes due to them, while reminding us that our commitment to God is also paramount. He invites believers to recognize God's sovereignty in their lives and to give Him their due, including worship, faith and obedience.

It should be noted that this phrase can be interpreted in different ways depending on the context and theological perspective. Some see it as an affirmation of the separation between state and religion, while others stress the importance of balancing earthly and spiritual responsibilities.

Chapter 2: Bible history of tithing

Tithing is mentioned in the Bible, more specifically in the Old Testament, notably in the book of Leviticus and the book of Numbers.

In the book of Leviticus, chapter 27, verses 30-32, it says: "All the tithes of the ground, whether of the crops of the earth or of the fruit of the trees, belong to the Lord; they are holy to the Lord." This means that people were encouraged to give 10% of their crops or income to God.

In the book of Numbers, chapter 18, verse 21, it is specified that tithes were intended for the Levites, who were the tribe in charge of religious service in ancient Israel. The Levites had no land to cultivate, so the tithes served as their financial support.

With its roots in the longest Christian tradition, the tithe remains the Church's primary resource today. In the Old Testament, there are several references to tithing, from Abraham's offering to Melchisedech to Jacob's offering to God.

St. Paul himself, addressing the Galatians, reminds us: "He who receives instruction in the Word, let him share out of all his possessions to the one who teaches him". While the sharing of wealth was pushed to a high degree in early Christian communities, the Church gradually established the practice of tithing from the Council of Tours onwards in 567. While Catholic practice has moved away from the radical etymology of the tithe or decime, from the Latin decima, which tended to represent a tenth of the resources of each believer, it has endured over time and merged into the denier du culte, created by the Church of France after the 1905 law.

"By offering these firstfruits, the people recognized that everything they had was a gift from God and that they were called to be faithful to Him in return."

3ème PART: TITHES AND OFFERINGS

3ème PART: TITHES AND OFFERINGS

Chapter 1: Beginnings

In the book of Deuteronomy, chapter 26 offers important theological instructions concerning first-fruits offerings. These instructions were intended for the people of Israel to guide them in their relationship with God and to remind them of their dependence on His providence.

Chapter 26 explains how the Israelites were to present their first-fruits offerings to the Lord once they were settled in the Promised Land. Firstfruits were the first fruits of the earth, representing the best of their harvests. The Israelites were invited to bring them before the priest and offer them in thanks and gratitude to God.

By offering these first-fruits, the people recognized that everything they had was a gift from God, and that they were called to be faithful to Him in return. The presentation of first-fruits was also an occasion to remember Israel's history, their liberation from slavery in Egypt and the importance of the covenant between God and His people.

Chapter 2: Vows and offerings to the Lord

A theological explanation of chapter 27 of the book of Leviticus. This chapter deals with the laws relating to vows and offerings made to the Lord.

Leviticus is a book of the Bible that mainly contains the laws and instructions given by God to the people of Israel. In chapter 27, God gives specific guidelines on the vows and voluntary offerings the Israelites could make.

According to chapter 27, when a person made a special vow to the Lord, he or she had to offer a certain monetary value based on the priest's estimation. This value could vary according to age, gender and other specific criteria.

This practice of vows and offerings was a way for the people to express their devotion to God and offer something of value in return. It showed their commitment to God and their gratitude for His blessings.

Leviticus emphasizes the importance of commitment to God and the responsibility to keep His promises. It was a way for the people to show their faith and obedience to God.

"God promises to open the floodgates of heaven and pour out upon his people blessings in abundance if they obey this directive."

4ème PART: THE DONATION PROCESS

4ème PART: THE DONATION PROCESS

Chapter 1: Bringing the tithe to the treasure house

An important passage on tithing is found in the book of Malachi, chapter 3, verses 10-11: "Bring all the tithes to the treasure house, that there may be food in my house; so test me, says the Lord of hosts. And you will see if I do not open for you the floodgates of heaven, if I do not pour out upon you blessing in abundance. For your sake I will threaten him who devours, and he will not destroy for you the fruits of the earth, nor will the vine be barren in your fields, says the Lord of hosts."

In this passage, God exhorts His people to bring all tithes to the treasure house, in order to provide for the needs of God's house. He encourages them to test him, and promises to abundantly bless those who are faithful in their practice of tithing.

God promises to open the floodgates of heaven and shower His people with abundant blessings if they obey this directive. He also assures them that he will protect their crops and prevent the destruction of their fruit.

This passage highlights the link between the practice of tithing and divine blessings. It is a call to trust in God and to be faithful in obeying His commandments.

Chapter 2: The Jewish approach to tithing

Tithing is a religious concept that requires the faithful to give a percentage of their income or possessions to the church or to a particular religious cause. However, tithing is more often associated with Christian tradition than with Jewish tradition.

In Jewish tradition, the concept of "ma'asser" or "Jewish tithe" exists instead. According to the Torah, Jews were required to tithe a portion of their agricultural income to the tribe of Levites and to the poor.

The approach to Jewish tithing varies according to individual practices and Jewish communities. However, the steps for tithing can be as follows: identifying income, separating the tithe, who receives the tithe and how to give it.

1. Income identification

Jews must identify agricultural income, such as produce, fruit, vegetables, animals, etc., which is subject to tithing.

2. Tithe separation

Once the income has been identified, the tithe must be separated. This usually involves taking 10% of farm income and setting it aside.

3. Recipient of the tithe

Jewish tithes must be given to the Levites and the poor. In contemporary Jewish communities, there are usually charitable organizations and religious institutions that act as intermediaries to distribute tithes.

4. How to donate

Giving arrangements can vary according to individual circumstances and preferences. Some people prefer to give their tithe directly to a specific beneficiary, while others choose to give it to an organization that will handle the distribution.

It's important to note that the practice of Jewish tithing can vary according to religious currents and individual interpretations. Some observant Jews follow this religious concept strictly, while others may interpret tithing symbolically or adapt it to their modern reality.

These tithing laws are important in the religious practice of Judaism, but they can vary according to the specific interpretations and customs of each Jewish community. This approach is broadly similar to that of Christians.

"Tithing is also observed on monetary income and property."

5ème PART: GOD'S PEOPLE AND THE TITHE

5ème PART: GOD'S PEOPLE AND THE TITHE

Chapter 1: Jews and tithing

Orthodox Jews continue to practice the laws of tithing, such as Terumah and Maasser rishon. Tithing, called "Ma'aser" in Hebrew, is a biblical Jewish concept that refers to the practice of giving a tenth of one's income or possessions to God. The law of tithing is derived from the Torah and is found mainly in the book of Leviticus.

According to Jewish law, certain agricultural products, such as grain, fruit and livestock, must be tithed. This means that a person must separate a tenth of his harvest or livestock and give it to the Levites (a specific tribe considered dedicated to Temple service) or to the poor. The Levite in turn would give part of what he received to the priests.

Tithing is also observed on monetary income and property. Some Jews donate a tenth of their income to charitable or religious institutions, while others use the funds to support social and community causes.

However, it is important to note that the practice of tithing is not universal among all Jews. Some may choose to give more or less than a tenth of their income or possessions, depending on their level of piety or personal interpretation of the law.

The Torah, the first book of the Hebrew Bible, contains several laws on tithing, which is the practice of giving a portion of one's income or crops to the temple or priests. Here are some of the most important laws on tithing:

Tithing is a divine commandment: in the book of Leviticus (27:30), it says: "All the tithes of the ground, of the crops of the ground or of the fruit of the trees, belong to the Lord; it is a thing consecrated to the Lord."

Tithes consist of the tenth part: The Torah specifies that tithes must be the tenth part of the harvest or income. In the book of Numbers (18:21), it says: "To the tribe of the Levites, Moses had given, by command of the Lord, the tithes which the Israelites were to give to the Lord."

Tithes are for the Levites: Tithes were intended for members of the Levite tribe, who were priests and temple servants. In the book of Numbers (18:24), it says: "The Levites shall receive tithes from the Israelites in payment for the service they perform in the tent of meeting."

Tithes must be offered regularly: The Torah specifies that tithes must be offered regularly, according to harvest or income. In the book of Deuteronomy (14:22), it says: "Every year you shall set aside the tithe of all the produce of your sowing, of all that your field brings in."

Tithes can be eaten: The Torah allows those who give tithes to eat them in the presence of the Lord. In the book of Deuteronomy (14:23), it says: "You may exchange them for money; but when you come to the place that the Lord your God will choose to make His name dwell there, you shall spend the money on whatever you wish: oxen, sheep, wine or strong liquor, whatever pleases you. And you shall eat there in the presence of the Lord your God, and you shall rejoice, you and your household."

Chapter 2: Christians and tithing

Tithing is a concept inherited from the Hebrew tradition, where the faithful are called upon to give 10% of their income or crops to the temple or Church. In Christianity, tithing is seen by some as a duty to financially support the Church and its ministries.

Christians who support tithing often believe it's a way of showing their gratitude to God for the goods He has given them, as well as investing in the Church's mission. They see it as a form of worship and response to God's generosity toward them.

On the other hand, there are Christians who do not practice traditional tithing, arguing that the New Testament does not specifically prescribe tithing as an obligation for believers. They believe that giving financially to the Church should be a voluntary act, based on personal conviction rather than religious obligation.

It's worth noting that some churches teach tithing strictly and insist on its importance, while other churches take a more flexible approach to financial giving. Finally, the practice of tithing varies according to individual Christian beliefs and convictions.

Tithing, the act of giving 10% of one's income to the church, has a significant impact on the lives of Christians in a number of ways:

Faith and trust in God: Tithing is an act of faith and trust in God, because Christians believe that everything they own is a gift from God. By giving 10% of their income, they show that they recognize that everything comes from God, and that they trust Him to provide for their needs.

Worship and gratitude to God: Tithing is a form of worship and adoration of God. Christians see this act as a way of showing their gratitude to God for His blessing and provision in their lives.

Supporting the church and its activities: Tithing is used to fund the church's activities and ministries, such as building maintenance, pastor and staff salaries, church programs, charities, etc. Christians therefore see tithing as a way of supporting God's work and contributing to the advancement of His kingdom.

Stimulating generosity: The practice of tithing encourages Christians to be generous and to give beyond the 10%. By tithing regularly, Christians develop an attitude of generosity that also manifests itself in other aspects of their lives, such as giving to the needy and volunteering.

Managing finances: Tithing obliges Christians to consciously manage their finances and prioritize their spending. By tithing, they must adjust their lifestyle and spending in line with this choice.

Spiritual growth: The practice of tithing can contribute to the spiritual growth of Christians, helping them to develop greater trust in God, cultivate humility and strengthen their commitment to their faith.

However, it is important to note that tithing is not an absolute obligation for all Christians, and the way it is practiced may vary according to the beliefs and traditions of each church or individual. Some Christians may choose to give more or less than 10% of their income, or to give other types of contributions, depending on their discernment and financial situation.

"No one can serve two masters. For either he will hate the one, and love the other; or he will cling to the one, and despise the other. You cannot serve God and mammon."

6ème PART: CHOICE AND THE FUNDAMENTAL DECISION

6ème PART: CHOICE AND THE FUNDAMENTAL DECISION

Chapter 1: God or Money

In the Gospel according to Matthew, there are several passages where Jesus talks about the relationship between God and money. One of these passages is found in Matthew 6:24: "No one can serve two masters. For either he will hate the one and love the other; or else he will hold to the one and despise the other. You cannot serve God and mammon."

In this passage, Jesus highlights the fact that it is impossible to serve God and material wealth at the same time. He points out that the love of money can become an idol that rivals our love and devotion to God.

Jesus invites his disciples to put their trust in God rather than in earthly riches. He teaches the importance of considering eternal and spiritual things as a priority over ephemeral material wealth.

Another relevant passage is found in Matthew 19:23-24:

"Jesus said to his disciples, 'I tell you the truth, it is hard for a rich man to enter the kingdom of heaven. Again, I tell you, it is easier for a camel to go through the eye of a needle than for a rich man to enter the kingdom of God."

In this passage, Jesus emphasizes the challenges wealthy people face in entering the kingdom of God. He points out that excessive attachment to wealth can hinder one's relationship with God and access to eternal life.

These passages highlight the importance of the heart's attitude towards money, and the need to put God at the center of our lives rather than allowing ourselves to be dominated by the pursuit of material wealth. Jesus invites us to show wisdom and detachment with regard to money, so that we can serve God with a sincere and generous heart.

Chapter 2: Tithing: the way to wisdom, discernment and happiness: GOD

Tithing is the religious practice of giving a tenth of one's income to a church or religious institution. It is present in several religions, notably Christianity and Judaism.

In Christianity, tithing is often associated with the notion of gratitude to God and the responsibility of believers to give financial support to the church and its ministries. It is seen as an act of faith and trust in God, who will provide for all the needs of those who give to Him.

Tithing is often interpreted as a way of showing gratitude to God for the blessings He bestows, and of participating in God's work on earth. It is seen as an act of generosity and a means of supporting religious actions, such as maintaining places of worship, helping the needy, spreading the Gospel, etc.

Some teach that those who tithe can expect to be blessed by God, both financially and spiritually. However, this belief is debated and interpreted differently within different Christian traditions.

It should be emphasized that tithing is a personal matter and each individual is free to choose whether or not to practice this form of giving. The essential thing is to give voluntarily, with a grateful and generous heart towards God and towards others.

Tithing is seen in some religious traditions as a path to wisdom, discernment and happiness, by showing gratitude to God and actively contributing to His work on earth. However, it is important to respect individual choices and not to impose this practice on others   .

"It's important to note that tithing for entrepreneurs and in business is a personal and voluntary practice."

7ème PART: ENTREPRENEURIAL AND BUSINESS TITHING

7ème PART: ENTREPRENEURIAL AND BUSINESS TITHING

Chapter 1: Tithing as entrepreneurs, businesswomen and businessmen

It should be noted that tithing is a practice specific to certain religions and is not compulsory for all entrepreneurs, businesswomen and businessmen. Everyone is free to decide whether or not to tithe according to their own beliefs and personal convictions.

Because of your loyalty, your heavenly Father promises you blessings far greater than your sacrifices. Tithing is a sign of our faith in Jesus Christ. If you trust in Him, you will be strengthened, guided and supported in your life to the extent of your needs.

Tithing is the religious practice of giving 10% of one's income to a church or religious organization. Traditionally, this practice is associated with the tithe paid by the faithful to support clergy and church activities.

In the context of entrepreneurs and business, tithing can take on a different meaning. Some people consider that giving 10% of their income to religious or charitable causes is a modern form of tithing. This practice can be seen as a way of expressing gratitude to God for the success of one's business, and sharing that success with those in need.

Other entrepreneurs may choose to contribute financially to religious or charitable organizations as part of their corporate social responsibility. For these entrepreneurs, regularly donating a certain amount of money to religious or charitable causes is a way of giving back to the community and supporting initiatives that match their values.

It's important to note that tithing for entrepreneurs and in business is a personal and voluntary practice. Each entrepreneur is free to decide whether and to what extent he or she wishes to donate part of his or her income to religious or charitable causes.

Chapter 2: The difference between philanthropic giving and tithing

Philanthropic giving and tithing are two types of giving, but they differ in origin and purpose.

Philanthropic donations are voluntary gifts made by individuals or organizations with the aim of improving society or supporting causes close to their hearts. Philanthropic donors can choose to support initiatives in fields such as education, health, the environment, arts and culture, research, etc. These donations are often motivated by altruism and the desire to make a positive difference in the world.

On the other hand, tithing is primarily a religious concept, dating back to the Old Testament of the Bible. According to this tradition, believers are encouraged to give 10% of their income or possessions to the church or a religious organization. Tithing is often seen as a religious duty and a way of supporting church activities, including priest or pastor salaries, building maintenance, social programs, etc.

The main difference between philanthropic donations and tithing lies in their origin (altruistic or religious motivation) and purpose (improving society or supporting a religious organization).

1. Testimony on tithing

This testimonial we're sharing with you comes from an awareness and training platform on tithing issues.

"This message is not intended to tell you what to do or not to do. I simply testify to my personal experience during 2015 when, for the first time in my life, I paid my tithe every month.

I've experienced two extremes when it comes to tithing, starting with what I call legalism, where tithing is not questioned: you have to pay 10% of your monthly salary, there are no exceptions. The churches that preached this way were not short of resources; they even lived in a form of material opulence (thick cushions on all the pews, that's a sure sign). The question I asked myself was: should I pay my tithe gross or net? Before or after tax deduction? Do I have to pay it on my 13th salary as well? And if I receive money as a gift, do I have to pay it on that money? So many questions arising from this legalism, so I had settled the question by simply not paying it.

Then I changed churches, and I reached another extreme: no obligation, everyone gives according to their heart. As a result, the church lacked resources, and I realized that managing finances was often a balancing act. As a result, I decided to pay my tithe at that time, to help out. So, when I was under a legalistic system at the start of my Christian life, I felt free not to pay, and when I entered a free system later on, I felt so obliged my conscience was working on me. So I started paying 10% of my net salary. But I soon ran into a major problem: when I calculated the amount I had chosen to pay each

Sunday, I soon calculated, somewhat in spite of myself, how much each minute of worship cost me. Suffice it to say that when minutes were wasted unnecessarily, in moments of adjusting the lectern or preparing the holy scene, I began to stomp my feet. At the price I was paying per minute of worship, I wanted my money's worth!

Of course, that system cracked pretty quickly and I stopped paying tithes. Definitely, I thought. At the same time, I increased my donations to various charities or to the poor, but without calculating a percentage, in order to compensate, and not to fall in love with Mammon. I told myself that if I added up all my donations over the year, I might end up with an amount close to the tithe. I may have reached it, but I'm not sure I've passed it.

Nevertheless, it was several years after this experience that I came across a training course given by Kurt Buehlmann on Top Chrétien, "40 days to revolutionize your finances" and once again reviewed my position.

Before going any further, I can't recommend this course highly enough to every Christian, poor, rich or in between. Its author combines astonishing pragmatism with astonishing faith, and the result is astonishing. I didn't come away unscathed; this training really revolutionized the way I managed my money. Its title, far from being a marketing gimmick, describes exactly what you'll find.

So, in March 2015, I decided to do the tithe test and give it all year round, retroactive to January 1. It's worth noting that at the same time, I quit my job on December 31 of the previous year to embark on a great entrepreneurial adventure. As a result, my income dropped to 35% of what it was in 2014, i.e. two-thirds less. Giving my tithe at a time when we're all having to tighten our belts was a daring gamble! But I stuck to it, throughout 2015. There were three months with no tithing, since there was virtually no income. A friend said to me, "It's easy for you to give now when you have next to nothing, but when your business is running and you're collecting big bucks, you'll change your stance!". It's both a profound encouragement (he thinks my business will bring in big bucks!) and a challenge for me not to stop depending on the size of my income.

The outcome of this experience is as follows: at no time did I lack for anything. I sometimes crossed the red line on my account, but everything quickly returned to normal. ...Another pleasing idea was this: we're just passing through, and nothing material belongs to us. In the end, we'll leave without being able to take anything with us. God has placed us here as stewards, and our mission is to take care of what he has placed at our disposal, whether it's nature, the animals, the people around us, or the money in our bank account. So, all this belongs to God, and yet he leaves us the usufruct of it.

When I think that in a country very close to mine, the state demands up to 80% of certain large salaries, and that I have the privilege of having a God who owns 100% of our salaries but only demands 10%, and with no obligation to pay! And on top of that, he gives us back this 10% afterwards, since part of the tithe is used to make great and beautiful feasts (yes, it's biblical).

As this tithing experiment has been perfectly conclusive for me this first year, I'm therefore renewing it with great pleasure in 2016 and will be back for a second review in twelve months' time.

God invites us to "put him to the test, to see if he won't open the floodgates of heaven". It's up to us to take him at his word!" Testimony of a General Manager, January 26, 2016

2. Examples of philanthropic giving by entrepreneurs

2.1 Andrew Carnegie's philanthropy and donations

Andrew Carnegie, one of the most influential captains of industry in American history, brought his philanthropic gifts to bear by donating much of his wealth to philanthropic causes. Carnegie firmly believed in the responsibility of the wealthy to use their fortune to improve society. So, in 1911, he created the Carnegie Corporation of New York, a foundation that continues today to support educational, scientific, cultural and social initiatives. Some of the most famous institutions funded by Carnegie include the Carnegie Libraries, Carnegie Hall and Carnegie Mellon University. These philanthropic gifts have had a significant impact on education and culture in the United States, and are still widely recognized and appreciated today. Through its philanthropic gifts, Carnegie has left a lasting philanthropic legacy that continues to help future generations.

2.2 Warren Buffet's philanthropic actions and donations

Another example of a world-renowned entrepreneur making philanthropic donations is Warren Buffett, the American billionaire investor and philanthropist. In 2006, Buffett announced his intention to donate over 99% of his fortune to charity, mainly through the Bill & Melinda Gates Foundation. His method of giving is based on a regular contribution of his shares in Berkshire Hathaway, the company he founded and runs, a portion of which he donates each year. In doing so, Buffett is widely praised for his commitment to philanthropy and for his influence on other wealthy entrepreneurs to follow his example.

2.3 Marc Zuckerberg's philanthropic actions and donations

Another example of a billionaire entrepreneur giving philanthropically is Mark Zuckerberg, the co-founder and CEO of Facebook. In 2013, Zuckerberg and his wife Priscilla Chan announced that they would donate 99% of their Facebook shares, worth tens of billions of dollars, to their foundation, the Chan Zuckerberg Initiative. This initiative aims to promote equal opportunities in education and health, and to support scientific and medical research. Zuckerberg and Chan's decision to donate a large part of their wealth has been widely praised for its commitment to the well-being and betterment of society.

3. Seven things every Christian should know about tithing

3.1 Tithing means a tenth or ten percent of your income.

Dekate is the Greek word translated as "tithe" and means "the tenth" or "ten percent" of everything you have.

3.2 Tithing represents the first fruits of everything you have.

The words "tithe" and "firstfruits" are used interchangeably, and there are several examples in the Bible. This is important to know because the word "firstfruits" is more commonly used in New Testament language. Because the word "firstfruits" is more commonly used in the New Testament church, some people mistakenly believe that the concept of tithing is an Old Testament Jewish practice that doesn't apply today.

Below are four examples of how the word "tithe" is replaced by the word "firstfruits" in the Old Testament. This proves that tithing represents the same thing as firstfruits.

3.3 The tithe is God's property. It's money that actually belongs to God.

Leviticus 27:30 "Every tithe of the land, whether of the crops of the earth or of the fruit of the trees, belongs to the Lord; it is a thing holy to the Lord."

3.4 Tithing is holy money, and anyone who misuses it is profaning a holy thing.

Leviticus 27:30 "Every tithe of the land, whether of the crops of the earth or of the fruit of the trees, belongs to the Lord; it is a thing holy to the Lord."

3.5 The tithe is used to support the priests.

Numbers 18:22-32 "The children of Israel shall not come near the Tent of Meeting any more, lest they bear sin and die. 23: The Levites shall minister in the Tent of Meeting, and they shall remain burdened with their iniquities. They shall have no possession among the children of Israel: it shall be a perpetual law among your descendants..."

3.6 There are 7 different types of tithes.

A tithe of cattle and herds of sheep and oxen;

A tithe of the fruits of the field;

A tithe from industries that produce oil, wine and wheat;

A tithe of the smallest possessions;

A tithe from the children;

A tithe of tithes.

3.7 If the tithe is ever used, it must be repaid with interest.

Leviticus 27:30-31 "Every tithe of the land, whether of the crops of the earth or of the fruit of the trees, belongs to the Lord; it is a thing consecrated to the Lord. 31: If anyone wishes to redeem anything from his tithe, he shall add a fifth to it."

4. Six reasons why those who don't tithe become poor

4.1 Those who don't tithe are impoverished because they have nothing to harvest.

Hosea 8:7: "Because they have sown the wind, they will reap the whirlwind; They will not have an ear of wheat; What grows will not yield flour, And if there were any, strangers would devour it."

4.2 Those who don't tithe are impoverished because they don't attract blessings on their lives

Malachi 3:10 "Bring to the treasure house all the tithes, That there may be food in my house; Put me thus to the test, Says the Lord of hosts. And you shall see if I do not open for you the floodgates of heaven, If I do not pour out upon you blessing in abundance."

4.3 Those who do not tithe are impoverished because they are cursed.

Malachi 3: 8-9 "Does a man deceive God? For you deceive me, And say: In what have we deceived you? In tithes and offerings...!"

4.4 Those who don't tithe are impoverished because devourers constantly eat their riches.

Malachi 3:11 "For you I will threaten him who devours, and he will not destroy the fruits of the earth for you, nor will the vine be barren in your fields, says the Lord of hosts."

4.5 Those who don't tithe are impoverished because the fruits of their fields are constantly destroyed.

Malachi 3:11 "For you I will threaten him who devours, And he will not destroy the fruits of the earth for you, Nor will the vine be barren in your fields, says the Lord of hosts."

4.6 Those who don't tithe get poorer because they lose their fruit before they have a chance to reap.

Malachi 3:11 "For you I will threaten him who devours, And he will not destroy the fruits of the earth for you, Nor will the vine be barren in your fields, says the Lord of hosts."

"More than an act of generosity, the denier is proof of every Catholic's involvement in the life of the Church."

AN OPENING ON THE DENIER DE CULTE

AN OPENING ON THE DENIER DE CULTE

In this section, we'll look at the denial of worship among Catholic Christians.

1. Background to Catholic Christianity

In the context of Catholic Christianity, it is not appropriate to speak of "denial of worship". Catholics practice religious worship centered on the celebration of Mass and the sacraments, and have a deep devotion to the Virgin Mary and the saints. They believe in the real presence of Jesus Christ in the Eucharist, and worship him at mass.

However, it is important to note that Catholics do not venerate or adore Mary and the saints in the same way as they do God. They ask for the intercession of Mary and the saints, that is, they pray for their support and intercession with God. Praying to Mary and the saints is a way of asking for their help and intercession, but adoration is reserved exclusively for God.

It's also worth pointing out that not all Catholic Christians practice their faith in the same way. There may be variations in religious practices and particular devotions according to local cultures and traditions in different parts of the world.

The Catholic Church is present in the lives of its faithful, both on a daily basis and in times of crisis. Whether it's providing young people with the guidance they need to build their lives, accompanying adults and families on the path of life and faith, or supporting people weakened by illness... these are all priceless missions, but they do come at a cost.

2. Origin of the denial of worship

Created by the Catholic Church in France after the separation of Church and State in 1905, the "denier du clergé" was instituted to cover the salaries of priests, which until then had been paid by the State. The State could no longer subsidize religious denominations. In Alsace-Moselle, these salaries continue to be paid.

This collection from the faithful was then called the "denier du culte", a term still often used, and since 1989 has become the "denier de l'Église".

The term "Denier" is a little outdated, but Catholics are keen to keep it, because the Denier is not a donation like any other. It doesn't appeal to generosity, but rather to a sense of belonging or fidelity to the Church, so that those who are more specifically in charge of proclaiming the Gospel and bringing the Church to life can be fairly remunerated. The "Denier" is a voluntary donation - there's no rate! Everyone gives according to his or her conscience and ability.

3. Denial of worship: Definition and usefulness in the Church

The "denier de l'Église" is therefore a voluntary contribution by Catholics, who in so doing express their belonging to the Church and their desire to help bring it to life. It is the dioceses' main source of resources.

The Code of Canon Law states: "The faithful are bound by the obligation to provide for the needs of the Church, so that it may have what is necessary for divine worship, for works of apostolate and charity, and for the honest sustenance of its ministers" (cf. canon 222 § 1).

The denier du culte is the financial contribution to the material life of the Church. Contrary to popular belief, the Church is not immune from need. Only the donations of Catholics enable it to survive, and to pay the salaries of its priests and lay employees. Donor support is essential if the Church is to continue its work.

The Denier is not enough, and only covers a significant proportion of expenses. Dioceses, parishes and priests have other resources to draw on, principally quests, ceremonial and mass offerings, bequests and donations. It is these revenues, taken together, that enable the Church's pastoral needs to be financed.

In almost all dioceses, however, the Denier is the most important component. It is therefore important to inform donors of the Church Pence of the preferred use of their donation: salaries, social security contributions, training, accommodation and expenses for priests and lay people on mission.

Saint Paul to the Galatians 6-6: "He who is taught the Word, let him give of all his possessions to the one who teaches him". Again, in the First Letter to the Corinthians (1 Cor 9:10-14), Saint Paul says: "If we have sown spiritual goods for you, would it be excessive to reap material goods?

In Matthew's Gospel, Jesus tells us that "the laborer deserves his wages" (Mt 10:10). This contribution is in line with both canon and civil law. Canon 222 § 1 states that "the faithful are bound by obligation to provide for the needs of the Church, so that it may have what is necessary for divine worship, for works of apostolate and charity, and for the honest sustenance of its ministers."

"By investing in the Kingdom of Heaven, we invite divine blessings to pour into our lives and the world around us."

CONCLUSION

CONCLUSION

The book "Tithing: Invest in the Kingdom of Heaven" offers a profound and inspiring perspective on tithing as an investment in the Kingdom of Heaven. It reminds us that, while the idea of giving 10% of our income may seem daunting at first, it's actually an opportunity to sow seeds of blessing and spiritual prosperity.

Through numerous biblical examples and personal testimonies, the author shows how tithing can not only help strengthen our relationship with God, but also benefit from His many blessings.

By explaining that tithing is an investment, this book invites us to look beyond the simple act of giving money and see it as a way of actively participating in God's work.

He emphasizes the importance of giving consciously, with gratitude and generosity, recognizing that everything we have comes from God. By sowing these seeds of faith, we pave the way for abundant harvests in our spiritual and material lives.

He encourages believers to seize the opportunity to intentionally and generously sow into the Kingdom of God. It reminds us that tithing is an act of faith and an instrument of blessing, which not only nourishes our relationship with God, but also enables us to participate in His mission of giving back. By investing in the Kingdom of heaven, we invite God's blessings to flow into our lives and into the world around us.

"Bless the Lord, my soul, and forget none of His benefits!"

BIBLIOGRAPHY

- UNIVERSAL BIBLICAL ALLIANCE, The Bible, New Revised Edition, 2013

- Philippe Jacques, A l'école de l'Esprit Saint, Les Editions des Béatitudes, Société des Œuvres Communautaires, 1995

- Claude Nicolet, "Le monumentum Ephesenum et les dîmes d'Asie", Bulletin de correspondance hellénique, vol. 115, no. 1, 1991, pp. 465-480 (read online [archive]).

- https://www.power-of-money.org/fr/2016/01/26/la-dime-c-est-tout-une-histoire-temoignage

- https://africa.la-croix.com/quest-ce-que-le-denier-du-culte-pourquoi-doit-on-donner-a-leglise

- https://eglise.catholique.fr/archives/cooment-soutenir-leglise

- https://africa.la-croix.com/tribune-dime-biblique-catholique/ February 10, 2018

- Claude Nicolet, "Dîmes de Sicile, d'Asie et d'ailleurs", in Le Ravitaillement en blé de Rome et des centers urbains des débuts de la République jusqu'au Haut-Empire. Actes du colloque international de Naples, 14-16 Février 1991, Rome, École Française de Rome, coll. "Publications de l'École française de Rome" (no. 196), 1994, 215-229 p. (read online [archive]).

- Claude Nicolet, "Le Monumentum Ephesenum, la loi Terentia-Cassia et les dîmes d'Asie", Mélanges de l'École française de Rome. Antiquité, t. 111, no 1, 1999, p. 191-215 (read online [archive]).

- Roland Viader (dir.), François Menant et al, La dîme : Dans l'Europe médiévale et moderne, Presses universitaires du Midi, 2010 (ISBN 978-2-8107-0902-1, online [archive])
- Michel Lauwers (ed.), Valentina Toneatto et al, Tithing, the Church and Feudal Society, Brepols, 2012 (ISBN 978-2-503-54525-7, read online [archive])
- (en) John Eldevik, Episcopal Power and Ecclesiastical Reform in the German Empire: Tithes, Lordship, and Community, 950-1150, Cambridge University Press, 2012 (ISBN 978-0-521-19346-7)
- Dominique Ancelet-Netter, La Dette, la dîme et le denier : Une analyse sémantique du vocabulaire économique et financier au Moyen Âge, Presses universitaires du Septentrion, 2010 (ISBN 978-2-7574-0159-0, online [archive])
- Gérard Bollon, " La grève des dîmes dans la paroisse de Saint-Voy au xviiie siècle ", Cahiers de la Haute-Loire, Le Puy-en-Velay, 1988

By the same author (Editions Universitaires Européennes)

1. Overall performance of an industrial group
2. Audit methodology to add value to your business
3. A tool for controlling the evolution of your company's accounts
4. Leverage your company's profitability
5. Increase your company's sales
6. The impact of management consulting on business development
7. The keys to business development in the agro-industrial sector
8. The keys to business development in the transport sector
9. Business start-up and development
10. Method for diagnosing your company's financial management system
11. Climate Change & Corporate Strategy
12. Renewable energies: What's at stake for your company?
13. 16 ways to reach your goals
14. Entrepreneurship
15. Risk Management
16. Corporate Daily Flash
17. Finance for non-financial managers
18. Investing in companies
19. 12 Investment opportunities

20. The seven (7) keys to growing your business
21. Drawing up an internal audit plan
22. Financial control and profitability
23. Seven (7) golden rules of profitability
24. Seven (7) benefits of artificial intelligence for your business
25. Digital transformation of financial management
26. Fossil fuel phase-out & corporate strategy
27. Sell More! Sell Better!
28. HR Management 2.0
29. AI revolutionizes business management
30. Resilience
31. Discernment
32. Bitcoin in the enterprise
33. Green finance
34. Green investments

The first twenty-eight (28) books are available in seven (7) languages, including French, English, Spanish, German, Italian, Portuguese and Russian.